The Super Organizer's Power of Consistency: Unlocking Positive Results

By James Lott Jr AFIS CTACC CDC
PMO OA CNA DD
The Super Organizer LLC
A Lott of Help
JLJ Media

People ask me many questions regarding my keys to success but there is one question and KEY answer that I feel is super important to the success of my professional life (and personal life in certain areas).

James, what is one thing you have done that you think has made you successful?

Being Consistent.

Consistency.

Not stopping and starting.
Not doing something "every once in a while"
Pushing through the low numbers while building an audience and putting out that podcast once a week.
Writing and releasing a blog post everyday for 3 months.

Nine time Emmy Winner, The Late Ed Asner (Mary Tyler Moore Show, Lou Grant, Up) told me in one of our interview chats that not quitting and staying "on the road" is what kept him booked and busy up till his death in August 2021. And he was busy.

It doesn't matter what industry you are in or what your exact goals are, consistency is a major factor. So I am sharing some of my advice and knowledge with you. This isn't a big book. It's easy to read. I wish for you much stamina and resilence.

And success.

This book is dedicated to the students of life. Edcuation never ends. Seeking knowledge and answers to move up and up is always a great idea.

This book is dedicated to all of those who put in the work and hand in there even when the odds seem insurmountable.

This book is dedicated to people who have ideas and dreams and aspirations and are willing to work for them.

This book is dedicated to YOU.

Introduction

Consistency is a key ingredient for success in any endeavor. Whether it's pursuing personal goals, professional aspirations, or cultivating healthy habits, consistency plays a vital role in achieving positive results. It is the unwavering commitment and persistent effort that leads individuals towards their desired outcomes.

We will delve into the profound impact of consistency and explore how it can transform lives.

I. Defining Consistency:

Consistency can be defined as the steadfast adherence to a set of principles, actions, or behaviors over time. It involves showing up, putting in the work, and staying committed, even when faced with challenges or setbacks. Consistency is not merely a fleeting burst of effort; rather, it is a long-term commitment to progress and growth.

II. Harnessing the Power of Consistency

1. Building Momentum

2. Consistency builds momentum and propels individuals forward on their journey. By consistently taking small steps towards their goals, individuals create a positive momentum that helps them overcome obstacles and stay focused. This momentum generates a sense of progress, which fuels motivation and encourages further consistent action.

3. Establishing Habits

4. Consistency is the cornerstone of habit formation. When individuals consistently engage in specific actions or behaviors, these actions gradually become ingrained habits. These habits, whether related to health, productivity, or personal development, can significantly impact one's life and lead to positive outcomes. Consistency helps individuals push through the initial resistance and transform desired actions into automatic habits.

5. Developing Discipline

6. Consistency nurtures discipline, which is essential for success. It requires individuals to exercise self-control, make conscious choices aligned with their goals, and resist temptations or distractions. Through consistent practice, individuals develop the discipline necessary to overcome challenges, persevere during difficult times, and make consistent progress towards their objectives.

7. Building Trust and Reliability

8. Consistency breeds trust, both in oneself and in the eyes of others. When individuals consistently deliver on their promises, meet deadlines, and show up consistently, they build a reputation for reliability and dependability. This fosters trust among peers, colleagues, and clients, opening doors to new opportunities and collaborations.

9. Learning and Growth

10. Consistency facilitates continuous learning and personal growth. By consistently engaging in an activity or pursuing a goal, individuals gain valuable experience, refine their skills, and develop a deeper understanding of their craft. The process of consistent effort exposes individuals to new insights, challenges assumptions, and encourages innovative thinking.

III. Overcoming Challenges
Setting Realistic Expectations:

11. To maintain consistency, it is crucial to set realistic expectations. Unrealistic goals or overly ambitious plans can lead to burnout and frustration. By breaking down larger goals into smaller, manageable steps, individuals can ensure a consistent approach without overwhelming themselves.

12. Dealing with Setbacks

13. Setbacks are inevitable on any journey towards success. Consistency helps individuals navigate these challenges with resilience. Instead of viewing setbacks as failures, consistent individuals see them as learning opportunities, adjusting their strategies and moving forward.

14. Cultivating a Growth Mindset

15. A growth mindset is vital for consistent progress. By believing in their ability to learn and improve, individuals can maintain a positive attitude even in the face of setbacks. Embracing challenges, seeking feedback, and being open to new approaches are all characteristics of a growth mindset that supports consistency.

16. Building Support Systems

17. Having a support system can significantly enhance consistency. Surrounding oneself with like-minded individuals, mentors, or accountability partners provides encouragement, feedback, and support during challenging times. They can offer fresh perspectives, hold individuals accountable, and celebrate milestones together.

IV. Practical Tips for Cultivating Consistency):

1. Goal Setting

2. Establish clear, specific, and measurable goals that align with your values and aspirations. Break them down into smaller milestones and create an action plan to stay focused and consistent.

3. Prioritization and Time Management

4. Prioritize your tasks & allocate time effectively. Identify your most productive hours & create a schedule that allows you to consistently dedicate time to your goals.

5. Creating a Routine

6. Develop a consistent daily or weekly routine that incorporates your desired actions or habits. A routine helps build momentum and reduces decision fatigue by making certain behaviors automatic.

7. Tracking Progress

8. Regularly monitor and track your progress. This allows you to stay accountable, make adjustments when necessary, and celebrate milestones along the way, reinforcing your commitment.

9. Self-Care and Well-being

10. Consistency requires taking care of oneself. Prioritize self-care activities like exercise, adequate sleep, healthy eating, and mental relaxation to ensure you have the energy and focus needed for consistency.

Conclusion:

Consistency is a powerful force that can lead individuals to remarkable achievements and positive results. By embodying steadfast commitment, establishing habits, developing discipline, and embracing growth, individuals can harness the transformative power of consistency. Though challenges may arise, by setting realistic expectations, maintaining a growth mindset, and building support systems, individuals can overcome obstacles and stay on the path to success.

Embrace consistency as a guiding principle in your life, and witness the incredible impact it can have on your journey towards personal growth and fulfillment.

Here are some synonyms for the word "consistent":

- Steady
- Stable
- Uniform
- Constant
- Regular
- Reliable
- Unchanging
- Dependable
- Unwavering
- Persistent

Being all of those things is also part of the receipe for success. I might take out one of them like Unchanging. I know why its like word but change is sometimes essential to making it.

This is an add on to the Consistent conversation, being Persistent. The can go hand in hand. Here are my thoughts:

Being persistent is helpful in building something for several reasons:

1. **Overcoming Obstacles**: Persistence helps you push through challenges and setbacks that are inevitable in any building process. Instead of giving up when things get tough, a persistent approach ensures you keep going until you find a solution.

2. **Skill Improvement**: Consistently working towards a goal allows you to develop and refine your skills over time. This continual improvement leads to higher quality results.

3. **Incremental Progress**: Building something often requires making steady, incremental progress. Persistence ensures that you keep making those small steps forward, which accumulate into significant achievements.

4. **Learning from Failure**: Persistence allows you to learn from failures rather than being discouraged by them. Each failure provides valuable lessons that can be applied to future attempts, increasing the likelihood of success.

5. **Achieving Long-term Goals**: Many worthwhile goals take time to achieve. Persistence keeps you focused and motivated over the long term, helping you reach your ultimate objectives.

6. **Building Resilience**: Persistent efforts build mental and emotional resilience. This resilience not only helps in the current project but also equips you to handle future challenges more effectively.

7. **Gaining Respect and Trust**: Consistency and persistence earn the respect and trust of others. Whether in a team or working with clients, being reliable and steadfast can strengthen relationships and build a positive reputation.

8. **Seizing Opportunities**: Persistent individuals are often more attuned to opportunities that arise. By continually working towards your goals, you are more likely to recognize and capitalize on opportunities that can aid in your building process.

Okay. I will end here. I hope this little book and what is written in it is helpful to you. I wish you all the success you are looking for.

James Lott, Jr. CTACC CDC CNA CHOC PMO OA DD, Certified Professional Organizer, is the Founder/CEO of The Super Organizer, LLC and of the Online Network/Entertainment Company JLJ Media. He is a National Speaker/Teacher, and Certified Life Coach.

He runs a network of over 30 shows (audio and video) from himself and others on his JLJ Media Network!

9 years running, James has the only weekly Organizing radio show called THE SOS SHOW with James Lott Jr. James is also the author of over 60 books. He has several songs out about Organization and has been featured in Forbes magazine. You can follow him at alottofhelp.com. He can also be found everywhere @jameslottjr (all social media and streaming platforms).

Copyright JLJ Media 2024

JLJ Media
8939 Sepulveda Ave
Suite 110 #339
Los Angeles CA 90045

www.ingramcontent.com/pod-product-compliance
Lightning Source LLC
Chambersburg PA
CBHW072057230526
45479CB00010B/1124